Life of Faith

I0170482

hidden TREASURE

The Uncovering of Christ in You!

CHRISTIE AMOYO

HIDDEN TREASURE
Copyright © 2024 by Christie Amoyo

Scriptures taken from the Holy Bible, New International Version®, NIV®. Copyright © 1973, 1978, 1984, 2011 by Biblica, Inc.™ Used by permission of Zondervan. All rights reserved worldwide. www. zondervan.com The "NIV" and "New International Version" are trademarks registered in the United States Patent and Trademark Office by Biblica, Inc.™ Scripture quotations marked (NASB) taken from the Amplified® Bible (AMP), Copyright © 2015 by The Lockman Foundation. Used by permission. lockman.org.

Softcover ISBN: 978-1-4866-2387-7
Hardcover ISBN: 978-1-4866-2389-1
eBook ISBN: 978-1-4866-2388-4

Word Alive Press
119 De Baets Street, Winnipeg, MB R2J 3R9
www.wordalivepress.ca

WORD ALIVE
—P R E S S—

Cataloguing in Publication may be obtained through Library and Archives Canada

Contents

Dedication

I want to dedicate this book to my children, Daniel, Dominic, Cali, and Donovan. I want you to see Jesus in everything you are and everything you do. Especially in those times when you think life is hard, I want you to know that God is right there with you. He hears every prayer you pray and answers them. Don't be discouraged. God always has a good plan for you. He let me bring you into this world for this specific time. You are filled with the power of God Himself. Rely on Him. Live in His love every day. Change this world… I know you can!

Introduction

This book was birthed in my heart after sharing a recent message at our Sunday church service. The more I speak this message, the more revelation I get and the deeper it sinks into my own heart.

I've always told God that I am very simple, and He needs to spell things out for me plainly. What I've come to see in my own life is that God keeps taking me to the Scriptures and revealing things to me in very basic and practical ways, often giving me visuals to go along with them. Sometimes I feel like a child who's learning the basics of the Word, but then it becomes so easy to understand and share with others.

That's how the good news changes our lives and we then become able to share it and change the lives of others!

There is a treasure you have found that is worth everything—a treasure that has changed your life forever. It's time to dig it out and share it!

chapter one

Scripture

The kingdom of heaven is like treasure hidden in a field. When a man found it, he hid it again, and then in his joy went and sold all he had and bought that field.

—Matthew 13:44

I HAVE READ THIS SAME SCRIPTURE REPEATEDLY THROUGH THE course of my life. Then, one day, God gave me a new revelation of it. I felt unsure about what God was stirring in my heart until I saw its truth in my own life and testimony.

I've heard this scripture explained by many teachers, and even by Jesus a few chapters later when He breaks down the meaning of this passage. So I was a little bit surprised, to say the least, and even hesitant to speak about it, when God gave me this fresh revelation.

As I've said, I am a very simple person. I pray all the time for God to show me revelations of His Word. Oftentimes I'll see a picture in my imagination which God uses to reveal something to me. This isn't a super spiritual experience; it's just an honest and simple way in which God speaks to me. When He opens my eyes to see things in a different way, it's revolutionary and changes my life instantly. If God can get something in your head, it has the power to change you!

I desire greatly to have God speak and reveal His Word to me in deeper ways. The Bible isn't just some novel or good book to read. It has so many levels of revelation and inspiration for us. This is why you can read the same scripture over and over again only to one day have it speak to you like never before!

Reading this scripture recently caused me to reflect upon my own life. We're all on our own journey. No two journeys are the same, but there is a point in our lives when we are introduced to Jesus Christ and our lives are changed. I don't necessarily mean that it's some sort of radical change, but something happens inside us that we know to be right, honest, and genuine. Something happens in us that we can't ignore. It's something we want to explore.

Our minds may not be fully convinced of these new thoughts, these changes of heart, but we feel enough of a pull that we decide that God is real. We believe in Him. We make this subconscious decision that ultimately alters our lives and brings us onto the path of a new journey. Our destiny.

> WHEN YOU CHOOSE JESUS, YOU CHOOSE LOVE, FORGIVENESS, HOPE, AND PEACE. YOU UNKNOWINGLY CHOOSE LIFE MORE ABUNDANT, AS WELL AS SUPERNATURAL POWER AND AUTHORITY. YOU CHOOSE TO RECEIVE THE HOLY SPIRIT, WHO COMES TO LIVE INSIDE YOU EVEN IN YOUR IMPERFECTION.

When you choose Jesus, you choose love, forgiveness, hope, and peace. You unknowingly choose life more abundant, as well as supernatural power and authority. You choose to receive the Holy Spirit, who comes to live inside you even in your imperfection. This treasure you have found becomes your own priceless treasure which you hold on to in your heart.

Whether you fully appreciate the worth of this treasure, you are stirred on the inside and a new desire is birthed in you.

Finding this treasure brings confusion to your current situation, feelings, and thoughts. Because of your uncertainty, you may just decide to keep all this bottled up, keeping it in your heart until your head knows which steps to take next.

So you bury it.

Then one day, after much thought and contemplation, you realize that you can't deny that God is speaking to you. He speaks in many ways and your heart won't feel whole or complete until you do something about it.

What will it be?

Finally, you just can't live without knowing this God who chose you. So you take everything you have and everything you know and place it at the mercy seat of Christ.

That's when something exciting happens! You feel eager about your new life, your new adventure. The smile, boldness, and courage that comes over you causes you to look at your life and make some pretty big changes. Whether those changes involve taking action towards your predetermined plan or just making a new commitment, they kickstart your faith walk.

It then seems like you question every thought in your mind and every choice you make. Life just isn't the same as it was before. You're entering a whole new world.

This is the point in time when you decide to give it your all and not look back. You're not just going to dig back up that buried treasure; you're going to buy the whole land that you buried that treasure in. You take all that you have and give it. Why? Because the treasure is yours and it has more value to you than anything else in the whole world.

After buying the land and possessing the treasure, you see how it brings value to everything about you and everything you do. The land is rich because of the treasure it holds. And as you work your land, without painful toil or sweat (Proverbs 10:22), you can enjoy the fruit of your labour. The fruit you harvest grows to become more than you can ask, think, or imagine (Ephesians 3:20). You have so much that you have to share it with others. Your treasure is impacting the world around you! It has become your seed, and it will multiply thirty, sixty, and one hundred times (Mark 4:20).

A transition takes place within you. The Word of God, your treasure, becomes the final authority in your life. You have transitioned from the kingdom of darkness to the kingdom of light (Colossians 1:13–14). And because of this light, You cannot be hidden (Matthew 5:14).

chapter two

My Testimony

I HAD TO LOOK BACK AT MY OWN LIFE, THE SITUATIONS AND circumstances I lived through, to understand the absolute love of God and the weight of the treasure I had found. As I continued to read the passage from Matthew 13, I was reminded that through the uncertainty and pitfalls of my life I had found the hidden treasure. I hadn't known its true value when I first found it, but when I was ready to dig it up and own it God was able to drastically change every part of my life.

Not only does God promise us a more abundant life but the blessing I can live in is for myself and everyone around me in every situation.

I was two years old when my grandmother started to take me to church with her. She once told me of a time when I had been in her apartment and I began speaking in another language. She thought it must have been tongues. I remember seeing a dove in her kitchen window right before this took place.

I had many supernatural encounters when I was with my grandmother. When she prayed for people, they were healed. It just wasn't natural to see limbs grow and tumours spat out on the ground. I watched these things take place when I was very young, and the encounters never left my heart or my mind.

As I grew older, I had two different views of the world. When I visited my grandmother, she showed me this crazy faith side of life. And when I went home, I saw the effects that alcohol was having on my family. My mom and stepdad, whom I lived with, were alcoholics and my dad, who lived just down the street from us, was one as well.

After witnessing the destruction alcohol brought all around me, I made many decisions in my own heart to keep me from those same choices.

Although I have many great memories from my childhood, many other memories aren't good. I was the child who chose to put a smile on my face and make the most of every situation. I was the girl in school who worked very hard in every class, cherished my friendships, and put my heart into everything I did. Those things brought great rewards to me and filled my heart and mind with external happiness.

Throughout my teenage years, I really struggled in my mind. I had an awareness that some of the things to which I'd been introduced, and some of the actions of those around me, just weren't good. As a teenager I tried to pretend like I was having fun, when really I was just unsure, or even scared.

One day, my best friend from all the way back in Kindergarten asked me to go with her to her church's youth night. I'd had no idea that her family even went to church! After she had left our school, I had barely talked to her. We had made new friends and grown apart.

But when she called and invited me to church, I was really intimidated at the thought of going. And then I realized that this was the same church where my grandmother attended.

We were just getting our drivers licences, which made going to church together even "cooler." For these reasons, I started to feel excited about going and hanging out with her.

She ended up inviting me again, and again... and then one night, when she couldn't come, I even went and brought another friend of mine.

One particular night at youth group, when I was fifteen, I felt a tug on my heart to pray with the pastor's wife about my family. I'm not sure if I even believed that Jesus could or would answer my prayers, and I wasn't even sure how this whole prayer thing worked, but I prayed with her about my mom, stepdad, and dad and the situation I was living in.

I don't know what made me think that God would even answer my prayer. I hadn't been going to church very long. I also hadn't been choosing the right things to do with my own attitude or my friendships. When it came to experimenting with alcohol, drugs, and unhealthy relationships, I was making the wrong choices. I attended every party I could.

After we finished praying together, I felt a small glimmer of hope that put a smile on my face. Maybe God was going to do something... eventually.

One night I invited some of my friends over to my house for a sleepover. This was on a weekend when my parents had gone out, and when they came home they weren't in the greatest shape. I was really embarrassed at all their choices that evening—and when my friends left the following day, I let my mom know how mad I was.

That was the day my mom's ears were opened for the first time, and she heard everything I said. She later told me that something had awoken inside her and she came to her senses. That day, she decided to never drink alcohol again.

A few weeks later, my stepdad decided to stop drinking too. If Mom wasn't having it anymore, he didn't want it either.

What I didn't know until years later is that my dad had also stopped drinking at this time and enrolled himself in an Alcoholics Anonymous program. He never went back to drinking.

I didn't fully understand what God was doing, but I knew He had intervened somehow. I was really happy about my parents and our newfound faith. We all started to attend that same church where I attended youth. We had so many new experiences together—going to church as a family, getting baptized, and learning about God. It was finally setting us on the right track. I was very thankful that this new routine in our lives started to build a positive foundation for us. As a teenager, I needed to know that God was right there with me.

I didn't realize at the time that saying a simple prayer with the pastor's wife could have such an impact—not just for my family, but for me as well.

> I DIDN'T REALIZE AT THE TIME THAT SAYING A SIMPLE PRAYER WITH THE PASTOR'S WIFE COULD HAVE SUCH AN IMPACT——NOT JUST FOR MY FAMILY, BUT FOR ME AS WELL.

I knew in my heart and mind that I had found something completely amazing, something priceless and life-changing: I knew that God was real. He had heard my simple prayer and answered it.

Through the setups of my praying grandma and my obedient friend, I found my way into my own land and discovered the treasure hidden within it. The treasure that had been hidden for me to find at the right time.

God's time.

In our lives, we all experience moments that shake us to the core. They carry a certain weight. These are our defining moments. My defining moments came when I remembered the treasure that I had found, the treasure which I had buried, and then I chose to buy the land.

Going to church and Bible studies became a regular thing once my parents surrendered their lives to Christ. I was happy for them and the way our lives continued to change—but I was still going to the same school and had all the same friends as before.

I soon became two people: a churchgoing Christian on Sunday and a fun, crowd-pleasing, party girl the rest of the week.

Yes, my teenage years were very challenging for me. After my parents were saved, I would get out my Bible and read about Jesus turning water into wine. Bible stories like that one made me convince myself that maybe my actions were okay. But on Sundays I would go to church and feel condemned about the way I had acted. I always regretted the mistakes I was making.

After living like this for so long, I realized how imperfect and unworthy I was. It became easier to live like I wasn't a Christian at all. I made one mistake after another, and by the end of each day I wouldn't even want to admit that I was in the wrong; I would have already determined that I would do it all again tomorrow.

For a long time, I pretended that I was having fun at parties. That is, until the condemnation got the better of me and I didn't care anymore. I was in a cycle of defeat. I didn't want my friends to think they had lost me now that I was going to church, but the truth is that I wasn't the same person they thought they knew.

So I struggled. A lot.

When Grade Twelve came along, with all the planning and shopping for graduation, I seriously contemplated my future after high school. My friends all seemed to know what they were going to do. Most planned to attend the major universities in Winnipeg, where we lived. But nothing interested me.

I had a moment of clarity one day while speaking to my cousin who told me about a Christian College she was thinking of attending. Well, that stuck with me. I thought about it for weeks.

Finally, I asked her for the brochure. When I found out that they had great academics and a successful volleyball team, I was sold. I knew that this whole hamster wheel I was on wasn't taking me anywhere. I needed to think with my own head and heart. After all, Jesus was in my heart.

I didn't know how to deal with all that yet.

Without telling my friends right away, I informed my parents that I was going to not only register for this college but live there on campus as well. I had a lot of emotions to sort through and several big steps to take. I knew that this was the right decision for me. I had to break free from living a double life.

I felt good thinking about this college, and I also knew it was a step in the right direction. I needed to break away from this routine.

Eventually, I needed to let everyone know. So I slowly started to tell my friends about this college I had applied for. I was going to take its four-year business administration program and play volleyball. Still, I left out all the Bible course details.

Not long after this, I was faced with one of the most embarrassing and demeaning situations of my life. While out for ice cream with a few friends, not to mention a few nicer-looking prospects, I was questioned very bluntly about my choice of schools. Why would I want to go to a place like that? Who did I think I was?

My face turned red and all eyes were on me. Then my best friend piped up and turned against me as well. Ouch!

I told them everything, in a very unconvincing sort of way. I explained that I was a Christian and this was a Christian school, and my cousin was going to this college as well.

After that incident, I knew that I was losing some friends. It was sad.

Graduation came and I ended up getting a double scholarship to attend this Bible college. That was encouraging. By this time, everyone knew where I was headed. One of my well-respected teachers even came over and questioned me about my higher education choices.

Summer came around and I turned eighteen. This came with parties of all kinds, which brought on a lot of friend guilt. I knew that our friendships weren't going to be the same once I moved away to college.

I was right.

But while I was still with them, I decided that it was time to enjoy every minute, and that meant making every compromise. When you start to make some good choices in your life, it seems you're always faced with tougher and tougher decisions. Tougher situations and tougher people to face.

Then it happened. I went to one party too many.

My parents picked me up from a friend's house one Sunday morning and I looked and smelled awful. I knew that going to church was the right thing to do, but I felt like I was too unworthy to go into that building. I entered the doors with my parents, my head hanging low. I was so ashamed of myself. I just wanted to run away.

My parents' friends all came up to us and gave me hugs. They told me such nice things about how beautiful I was, and it couldn't have been farther from the truth—at least in my eyes.

I was so happy to get into our seats and away from the chaos. My head was spinning.

As the worship and music began, my stomach felt more nauseous by the second. Needing to leave, I ran into the washroom and got sick. Thankfully no one was in there. I had never felt so awful.

After a few minutes, I mustered up the strength to get over to the sink and look at myself in the mirror. That's when God spoke to me. Inside, as loud and clear as could be, I heard these words: *"You are becoming exactly what you hated."*

Well, God knew me. I hated the whole drinking scene and had vowed to myself as a young girl that I would never be influenced by that. And yet here I was. Standing in church, completely hungover, I had no other care in the world but myself. I was literally losing my mind.

These were the exact words I had spoken to myself all those years ago, and now God was the one reminding me of them. I believe He was showing me a glimpse of my future if I didn't change.

I washed my face and assured God that this wasn't going to be my future. From that moment forward, I changed forever. I left the washroom feeling much better and filled with revelation power.

God had chosen to speak to me, which meant He must care about me. I would seek Him and praise Him with my whole heart.

I went back into the service and sat beside my mom. She looked at me in a totally weird way and asked if I was okay. I told her that God had spoken to me, but I would tell her all the details after church. She looked to be in a bit of shock, but she knew God must have done something, for I had changed in a blink of her own eyes.

chapter three

Treasure Worth Seeking

I WAS REMINDED OF THE TREASURE I HAD COME UPON AS A teenager while praying to this unknown God. He had shown me that He was God, the only God, and then He answered my impossible prayer at the age of fifteen.

At eighteen years old, I remembered the treasure and valued it even more. This pivotal moment set me on a path to find out everything I could about this treasure, for I knew the treasure was worth seeking.

While in college, I met a lot of great people, my roommate being one of them. She was a little older than I, but she was someone I thought of as possibly being a "perfect Christian." She was very kind, respectful, and soft-spoken. She also read her Bible and prayed regularly. I decided to just watch her actions, responses, and character and learn.

There were other people in my grade who I was surprised would even call themselves Christians. They acted like nice church people during regular school hours but managed to sneak away and act like the rest of the world every weekend. I mean, I had already come from the worthless life of partying, drinking, and drugs—and here they were, involved in it all. I was a little confused by their actions. I had assumed that if you called yourself a Christian, it must mean that you'd had a real life-changing encounter like I had. I had so much to learn.

I made a good group of friends at college. I may have enrolled in business classes, but the classes that really grabbed my heart and attention were the spiritual formation and Bible courses. I wanted to know everything about this God who had chosen to change my life, answer my prayers, and speak to me!

During this time, I was researching this treasure I had found with my head and my heart.

I wasn't very satisfied with my first year of academics at college. I was frustrated that all the math courses I had thought I would love ended up being such a burden, and that all the business courses were a bit of a bore. I didn't want to quit going to school, though, so I transferred over to an education major instead. Again, I really enjoyed the Bible courses and excelled in those. The other courses just weren't as interesting to me.

During this year, I started to date the man I would marry. Thankfully this was an area in my life where I had made some important decisions before coming to Bible college. I already felt like I had made a lot of mistakes and wasted a lot of emotions on wrong relationships. After taking time with God to heal my heart and show me what a godly relationship would look like, I made the commitment that the next person I dated was the one I was going to marry. I had even made a list of all the things I really wanted in a future husband.

I was friends with Danrey before we decided to date. He was the funny, centre-of-attention type who came to all my volleyball games. For the whole first year of our friendship, I didn't think of him at all as a future husband; he was just someone I enjoyed hanging out with… and laughing with— or laughing at!

Without the thought of dating, you can really let your guard down and share your feelings about everything in life, and that's what we did. We were just us. I got to know a lot about him, and he got to know everything about me.

So when our second year of school together was underway, we naturally spent more and more time together, talking on the phone longer and longer and realizing that it felt weird when we weren't doing these things.

My friends started to tease me a bit and I would blush and deny it... but then I questioned my feelings for Danrey. I'm the type of person who can't drag things on and on without knowing the outcome, so I started the ball rolling.

> I WAS ON A MISSION TO LEARN EVERYTHING I COULD ABOUT GOD, AND I DIDN'T LIKE BEING DISTRACTED BY THOUGHTS AND FEELINGS THAT MIGHT LEAD ME ASTRAY.

I was on a mission to learn everything I could about God, and I didn't like being distracted by thoughts and feelings that might lead me astray. If he felt the same, great! And if he didn't, great! He already knew about the commitment I had made to God—so if he said yes to our relationship, then he might as well say yes to marriage. So much pressure!

What Danrey told me solidified our unofficial engagement. He told me I was genuine and that's what he loved about me. Every time I hear that word, *genuine*, I find that it holds so much meaning. He accepted me with all my flaws, mistakes, and shortcomings. Just like Jesus.

At the end of that year, I graduated with a diploma in Biblical and Theological Studies. I was very proud of that, even though it wasn't the business or education majors I had originally enrolled in. It reflected what I loved and the wisdom I was chasing.

I wanted to go on a missionary program but ended up working for a local Christian camp for a little while. Still unsettled about my choices, I ended up working for a small family-owned gift store, a job which I held for the next nine years. I also volunteered at our family church for a while and attended some of their fellowship groups.

Danrey still had a few more years of school to attend. He'd always had a clear vision about wanting to become a youth pastor and had his home church ready to take him on as soon as he graduated.

During the upcoming year, with him commuting back and forth to school and me being out of college, was a time of us trying to plan for our next few years.

I started to attend his church every now and then. It was completely different than the one I went to. It was almost entirely Filipino, with some preaching in Tagalog. This presented a challenge for this English-speaking Caucasian. The church was also very small. But when I first attended with him, it really captivated my heart. I was still so excited to learn about God, but however and wherever I could hear and learn about God, I would.

After his next year of school, we got engaged and then married right after his graduation. For our wedding, we did everything according to tradition. In fact, everything we were involved in was very traditional. Sometimes I think we just blindly agreed to so much in our lives because we assumed that doing stuff for God made us acceptable to Him. And if not to

Him, then it made us acceptable to everyone around us. These seemed like the Christian things to do.

Somehow my search for God began to get skewed with acts of service rather than seeking Him with my whole heart. Sometimes we just go through the motions without thinking about them. When there's a lot going on in our lives, we can forget about the treasure we found and what it means.

For nine years, Danrey and I both got trapped in an ugly cycle of service and defeat. Our marriage was in trouble, our family was in trouble, our health was in trouble, and our finances were in trouble. There had to be a way out of this mess.

The God who chose to speak to me became silent. Or maybe I just wasn't hearing His voice above the chaos and confusion. Maybe I liked calling myself a Christian, acting like this person others wanted me to be. I liked the approval I got, but inside I knew that this was not what I had signed up for.

I had lost all my high school friends by the time I left college and now I only had Danrey as my best friend and he wasn't pursuing God like I thought someone should who had grown up as a Christian. I wanted so badly to grow and learn and be like Jesus. But there always seemed to be something I had to do or another class I had to take that was supposed to get me closer to Him.

Thank God I had my grandma to look to. She hadn't grown up as a Christian and her life had been radically saved one day while I was just a baby. Not being able to read, she listened to the Bible on tape day and night. Her pursuit resembled my pursuit. But she walked in signs, wonders, and miracles. During this time in my life when I was seeking God best, I knew how it was that my grandma had been able to show me that there was more. Healing, deliverance, and the supernatural was her way of life.

What I didn't know was that my grandma had found this hidden treasure when she'd been saved. She had then given all she had. She'd stopped living any other way, in one moment, and lived God's way for the rest of her life. I know that her family questioned her, and sometimes it was hard for them to understand why she had begun to serve God. Maybe she just couldn't explain the things she had experienced or seen to everyone… but I loved to hear it. She had bought her field where the treasure was buried. That became her territory, and the treasure changed the value of the land.

When my children find a shiny rock on the ground, I see them clean it off in their hands so they can see it sparkle. The same is true with this hidden treasure. To find it, and appreciate its beauty, the dirt needs to be cleaned off.

chapter four

Real Life

DURING THOSE NINE YEARS OF WORKING FOR GOD, WE LOVED Him but were not hearing Him. The breaking point came in my life when I again came face to face with a decision that drove me into another realm. Maybe it was to another level.

If I hadn't recognized the disconnection we felt during that period of our lives, I think we would still be finding ourselves in the same situations repeatedly. When you're trying to live a Christian life and look to others more than you look to God for help, healing, or answers, this hamster wheel just keeps spinning. You get frustrated. You get tired. You feel hopeless. And you lose your vision.

We were told, "God has great plans for your life." But we thought that maybe we just weren't good enough to receive anything great.

We could see other people being blessed in their lives. Healing for some, nice houses for others, and all sorts of miracles. Deep down we hoped that God was going to remember us too and that we would have a testimony.

I was about to step into a realm that my spirit was preparing me for, a realm that my natural self couldn't handle on its own.

At this time, my husband and I had been married for five years and decided to have a baby. Maybe we were at a point when we too were feeling like something was missing. Like the next step in our relationship. But it could have also been the emptiness we exposed ourselves to in our marriage. We were busy people, working and doing and going and being constantly busy. We were still very selfish in our decisions and actions but enjoyed and loved each other at the same time.

I wish we could have turned back time and worked on our relationship and marriage more. We could have prioritized our own team and kept us healthy instead of wearing ourselves thin and giving each other the leftovers.

We got pregnant, started to share the good news with our family, and then went through a terrible pregnancy loss. I went into a state of depression. The smile on my face hid the pain in my heart. My husband couldn't understand the feelings and pain I was going through and I didn't really want to share it with him. I figured he just wouldn't understand, and I was the one who would have to get over it.

Before I was completely healed, we got pregnant again. This time everything in my pregnancy went by the books. Nothing out of the norm. We were on our way to our so-called "happy new life."

After our son Daniel was born, he joined us in our acts of service at the church. We tried to do everything as a family. He pretty much grew up in the church building and everyone there became his godparent.

His first year was amazing and eye-opening for us. We became very confused with the demands of parenthood and the demands of the church. If we weren't doing something in and for the church, we felt like we weren't pleasing God. And with a baby in tow, this became very difficult in our hearts and minds.

I felt stranded. My son and I were our own little island.

I was thankful to be home with him as much as I could, though, and this changing season in our lives gave me some clarity. I got to sit back and reflect on what I liked and disliked about my life. I started to really live for my son. If my husband had to work in the ministry, I could be the Proverbs 31 woman. I was determined to be everything I could as a caregiver and supporter in our home.

I'm thankful that during this time I also got back to journaling. I had time, during naps and long evenings alone, to write. I had always enjoyed my quiet devotional time, and with that came opportunities to write down my thoughts and prayers. I was reconnecting with God and didn't see that my husband and I were disconnecting all at the same time.

Soon a year had gone by and we seemed to hit another plateau. Danrey's work was steady and constant, and we thought maybe this would be a good time to have another baby. After all, the son we already had had brought us so much joy and distraction from the things that really weren't going too well in our lives.

I got pregnant but lost the baby at the eleven-week mark. This miscarriage was completely shocking and painful. I had already looked pregnant and it had seemed as though I could possibly be carrying twins. It took a really long time to "get over" this loss. It was hard to talk to God, or talk to anyone, about it. So I didn't. I just wanted to not feel the pain anymore. I wanted to hide.

My husband felt my pain, too, but he was also too busy to help with the healing process. We didn't really talk about it.

He continued to work, and I continued to be strong on the outside for our son and the congregation.

We were leaders in our church, praying for people and believing that God could perform miracles in our lives. I saw some healings take place and took part in some good fellowship times and worship services. God had me there for a reason. It was to accomplish His purpose, not my own.

After another year of distractions and everything else, we decided to try again for a baby. There was prayer and much hoping for something better... but then there was still more loss.

This time I was just mad. Mad at God and mad that I felt like I was wasting time. I wanted to be a mom to this amazing boy I already had, yet I had to miss Christmas with him because I was in the hospital again. I was furious.

Danrey didn't even know how to feel about it all. He just had a big hole in his stomach. It made us all sick to our stomachs to think about it.

In fact, no one knew what to say to us. No one really knew what we were going though. If anyone said anything to us, it just felt wrong. It hurt, and I didn't want to hear it. I wanted to just get on with our lives.

> NO ONE KNEW WHAT TO SAY TO US. NO ONE REALLY KNEW WHAT WE WERE GOING THOUGH. IF ANYONE SAID ANYTHING TO US, IT JUST FELT WRONG. IT HURT, AND I DIDN'T WANT TO HEAR IT. I WANTED TO JUST GET ON WITH OUR LIVES.

I was lost. Our marriage was beginning to really suffer from the lack of communication, intimacy, and oneness between us. Our finances were a mess, having deteriorated because we had neglected everything in our lives.

How could we get to a place of such disillusionment? We were good people, Christians who loved God and served Him in the church. Nonetheless, our lives seemed to be falling apart.

At this point, we tried doing everything we could to stabilize our finances. I didn't understand how much of an impact this had on my husband's well-being and mindset and he headed down a road of depression and anxiety. He worked a lot, which brought him the distractions he needed to avoid having to deal with our finances or the pressures of family life. The busier he became, the more we fell for the lie that everything would just work out in the end.

And we certainly came to our end. The end in our finances, our health, and our marriage. Couldn't God just do something that would change our situation and help us?

For nine years we had just believed that God would do what He wanted to do. We believed that some people hear from Him or receive miracles. We just accepted that we weren't those people.

I came to the end of myself when I went through a period of loneliness, despair, and child loss. This was not God's great plan for my life. I knew He never left me, but maybe the treasure I'd had found years earlier had just been a one-time answer to prayer.

That didn't sit right with me.

I didn't realize that the treasure I had found needed to be cleaned and maintained. I had to help it shine in my life. I had to see that it wasn't just something I had found; it had also found me.

The kingdom of God is like treasure that's been hidden. But it doesn't just get put up in a display case to be looked at every now and then; it's so powerful that once you touch it, it becomes part of you.

chapter five

Real God

ONE SUNDAY MORNING AT CHURCH, DANREY AND I WERE DOING our regular thing and preparing for the service when we were told that a last-minute guest pastor was coming and would be the one speaking that morning.

Little did we know that this was to be one of our defining destiny moments.

This preacher blew the socks off everyone in our church. His booming voice caught and kept our attention. And as he laid hands on people, or barely laid hands on them, they fell to the ground under the power of the Holy Spirit. He told people in the congregation messages that came right from God. I know this because we knew these people and he was absolutely correct in what he imparted to them.

Before he laid his hand on my forehead, I watched him move throughout the congregation in awe.

God, I'm a Christian too, I said in my spirit. *Why aren't I like him?*

My husband, because he was the associate pastor at the time, was told to take this preacher man out for lunch. The other leaders were going to meet up with us at the restaurant.

In awe, we brought him in our vehicle. Along with our son, we drove to the closest, nicest restaurant. This is where my treasure was uncovered again.

As we waited for our table, the preacher looked at our son and asked us if we were going to have any more children. I told him that we had just been though some horrible pregnancies and that we didn't want to try anymore.

The hostess brought us to our table and we sat down. This preacher sat across from me, looked into my eyes, and told me that we would have more. I was stunned at his bold statement. Up to this point, almost everyone around us had shared their pity, grief, and concern, encouraging us to not to try again.

This preacher was the complete opposite. He spoke out hope.

I sat with a blank stare on my face, not even looking at Danrey to check whether he was listening. The whole restaurant faded into the background as the preacher went on to tell me about his own son and daughter-in-law, who had gone through a scary and frustrating time during her pregnancy with twins. To everyone else, the situation had looked hopeless. But through faith in God and choosing to believe and speak life and good things over their circumstances, everything had turned around. While she was in the hospital, the doctors had been ready to terminate the pregnancy. On their final ultrasound check, though, they confirmed that some sort of miracle had taken place. Both twins were now healthy and out of harm's way.

The preacher asked if I knew why he was sharing this with me. I nodded and started to tear up.

"You will have more," he said again.

My tears of faith released. Yes, I cried in faith! His words confirmed what I wanted. I wanted God to change my situation. I wanted Him to shut the mouths of the lions and bring me out into victory.

I wanted the faith that this man was talking about. It seemed so simple, some kind of holy stubbornness. Maybe he was just confident.

Soon enough, the rest of the group from church joined us. We had a nice lunch, but my spirit was stirring the whole time.

The rest of the day, I couldn't stop thinking about what had taken place. In fact, my husband and I talked about it for the whole next month. We just had a feeling that we'd really been missing something until now, and this revelation was filling it in.

During this time, my husband was still battling within his own mind. He had come through a diagnosis of Bell's palsy and was always trying to figure things out and fix the stress and mental mismanagement in his life. But you can only carry that weight for so long.

After that preacher came and spoke hope into our family, we started listening to some of the faith preaching on TV. It was all very encouraging—and that's what brought us through this season of our lives.

> WHEN I GOT PREGNANT AGAIN, I KNEW THIS WOULD BE THE TEST.

When I got pregnant again, I knew this would be the test. How were we going to handle it and respond as every doctor went into panic mode and rushed to get me in to have an ultrasound? Every friend and family member stood in shock, politely not knowing what to say as we told them we were pregnant again. The fear was thick all around us.

As for my husband, it was hard for him to unlearn much of the religious thinking he had grown up with. He didn't speak much during this period. I knew he had hope and a new revelation of what and who God was, but he was smart not to speak his doubt or fear towards me or our unborn baby.

I held on to that new hope and the words I had received. I believed that God had used this man to speak to me and that there must be a reason behind it.

I kept listening to faith messages, but the true test came as our friends told us they were getting married and wanted us to perform their wedding—in Hawaii. Besides our finances being a bit of a mess, my husband was unsure about a lot of things in his life, and now we also were pregnant again, which might be a deal-breaker for this trip...

But we said yes anyway.

I kept telling myself that everything was going to work out. I had an ultrasound coming up shortly that would confirm everything. The doctor was expecting another operation, and even though I didn't feel like I was completely solid in the words I had received, I was expecting something to be different this time.

One thing that I did pray was that my baby was going to be in the right spot during the ultrasound and have a strong heartbeat. That was something I longed to hear and I kept declaring it over myself.

When the day of the ultrasound came, the technician went about the procedure as quiet as can be. She then told me that my doctor was on call... but then the technician looked at me and gave me the good news.

"Your baby is in the right spot and has a really strong heartbeat. Have a great vacation in Hawaii."

I was overwhelmed.

Well, we maxed out our credit cards and booked our trip to Hawaii.

The pregnancy provided a glimmer of hope for my husband too. He again didn't say much, but I knew he was happy about our pregnancy and surprised that we were able to take this trip. We had been married for seven years and never gone anywhere.

We definitely enjoyed that trip. Together, we were getting a new vision of what we wanted to see more of in our lives. This new revelation brought us so much peace in our marriage too.

After Hawaii, our marriage still wasn't perfect. The healing process in different areas of our lives was overwhelming, tiring, and painful at times. But I was invigorated with new faith and knew God was at work.

The pregnancy had its challenges, and a friend passed me some pages from a book that went with a series of declarations I could make, according to Scripture, over my baby and my body. I took those and spoke them often in prayer. I occasionally had some cramping, bleeding, and a whole bunch of mixed emotions as I was nauseous with this one for the entire nine months. Even when I was farther along in the pregnancy, people still didn't want to congratulate us or say anything positive… just in case something bad were to happen.

During this season, we had the opportunity to sell our house and get out of debt. We agreed that this was a great opportunity for us and moved back in with my parents until we found something new.

That's when my husband hit the lowest point in his walk through depression. For months he stayed in bed, ate very little, and just couldn't handle any more stress. But this was also a time when I wouldn't stop praying for and encouraging him. I tried to stay "normal" around him. I wasn't going to baby him, because I knew what he was capable of. I was also careful with my words, making sure they didn't condemn him during this time. After all, I was pregnant still, fighting my own faith battles and seeing them won day by day.

Sure enough, he started to read Joyce Meyer's *Battlefield of the Mind*, and soon he was able to pull himself out of that pit he was in. It wasn't something that changed overnight, but by thinking right thoughts about himself and God he not only regained his confidence to live life but eagerly desired it to be life more abundant.

At this point, we knew we were in for something huge. When our second son was born and we held him in our hands, we just knew that it was only by faith that we had him. We came out of the pit of desperation and despair. Hope was birthed. The promise was alive and well!

chapter six

Real Faith

Now to him who is able to do immeasurably more than all we ask or imagine, according to his power that is at work within us. . .

—Ephesians 3:20

THE HIDDEN TREASURE I'VE BEEN WRITING ABOUT IS THE LIVING promise that causes your hopes, dreams, and vision to take shape in every area of your life. And with that treasure, you might need more courage than faith.

Even when the incident with the guest pastor at our church was long over, I still couldn't shake the stirring in my spirit. God was showing me something and I couldn't settle. I was suddenly drawn to watching and hearing faith messages and preaching on TV. There just had to be more to this Christian walk than I was experiencing.

During this time, my mother came across her own revelation that caught her attention, in the form of kingdom teachings from Pastors Gary and Drenda Keesee. She thought I would like these teachings, too, so she passed them on to us. Because of our hunger to hear more of the Word, we listened to them over and over again. In fact, they are so good that we still, twelve years later, keep listening to them! They helped explain more of these questions we were beginning to have.

Why wasn't our faith working? Why did we struggle in life? Why did it seem like God answered some people's prayers and not all? If we worked for God, literally as pastors, why weren't our needs being met? And so on...

We started to get real answers for our faith, family, and finances.

What was happening in my spirit? The same God who had answered my prayer at age fifteen and spoken to me at eighteen was actually showing me that it was time to take that treasure to the land it was on. The land was my whole life.

God didn't want to be part of just some of my life, the good religious part; He was teaching me how He was relevant to my *whole* life. Every single part of it. He wanted to show me that He was part of my healing process—for my mind, body, and spirit. He wanted to affect every area that affected me, physically manifesting as I gave Him access to my life.

Yes, I was learning that I had to give God access to work in my life. He couldn't just come in and overpower me in every area, especially if I hadn't given Him access to it by believing that He can and it's His will for me.

So many times, I didn't believe that God cared about answering my prayers when so many other people in the world needed His help as well. If my situation was desperate enough, I thought maybe God would intervene. This is wrong thinking.

I also read His Word and thought it sounded nice and hopefully it meant something good for my life. Someone had once told me that God was sovereign, that He knows what He's doing, meaning that when bad things happened to me, it was His plan and will. I also heard people say that faith and reality are two separate things.

That, too, is all wrong.

I began to realize that I had listened to and believed a whole bunch of lies. I needed to hear more encouraging words, see God as always been true to His Word, and start hoping for my future.

Hope is a word people use very loosely, but it has an amazing truth behind it. We often find ways to dumb things down, to take their power away, and in doing so the truth loses all its effectiveness in our lives. Hope is about having a confident expectation in the Word of God. Can I stand on God's Word and His character with confidence? Can I say that God's Word is final and true all the time? That's what we declare when we say that we have hope in God. We're confidently expecting Him to change our lives.

> I BEGAN TO REALIZE THAT I HAD LISTENED TO AND BELIEVED A WHOLE BUNCH OF LIES. I NEEDED TO HEAR MORE ENCOURAGING WORDS, SEE GOD AS ALWAYS BEEN TRUE TO HIS WORD, AND START HOPING FOR MY FUTURE.

That's what living by faith means. I walk in the confident expectation that God is going to do what He said He's going to do. I agree with His Word. And I'm not going to back down when frustration, confusion, and persecution come my way because my mind is fully convinced and I am fully confident in who Christ is.

I also had to hear and keep hearing the Word of faith being spoken. I had to get around faith-filled believers to see how they were living and speaking.

During my husband's healing process, I was on maternity leave. We listened to faith teachers, one after another. It was the uncompromised Word being preached by people like Kenneth and Gloria Copeland and Joyce Meyer. We also played Gary and Drenda Keesees CDs continuously in our vehicle. These preachers were so encouraging that they caused us to dream bigger. They read the Word and believed what it said. And as they walked it out, they saw it happen in their lives.

That seemed too easy and too good to be true. Yes, they too faced difficulty and frustration, but it had brought them to a point where they surrendered everything and trusted God wholeheartedly. And now they had become hugely effective teachers with ministries all around the world.

As we listened to their testimonies, we realized that we were so similar in the things we had faced and were climbing out of. The same struggles they had gone through were some of ours. They just had the fruit to show from their years of believing and walking out their faith. Now they were able to impact people.

The difference I saw immediately in our lives was that our hope was rising. As Isaiah 40:31 says, *"[B]ut those who hope in the Lord will renew their strength. They will soar on wings like eagles; they will run and not grow weary, they will walk and not be faint."* We started to have a different kind of strength and energy full of God's peace and joy. Our attitudes and speech changed. We started to look different, too, and others took notice. Ministry became exciting, for it was hard not to share about God's goodness in our lives.

We were overwhelmed.

A fire had been lit inside us as we pondered everything we had walked through that year and the victory we had experienced. So many different areas of our lives were being affected as we stepped out in faith.

That treasure I had found when I was fifteen years old and hidden in the ground was the same treasure I needed to dig back up. For fifteen years I hadn't known the true impact of this treasure.

Until now. Now was the time.

But I couldn't just dig up that treasure, for it had been planted in the ground on purpose. It had roots. I needed to buy the land it was on and own it.

This was the revelation God gave me for this book. At some point, we all come across this treasure. Although we think it's beautiful, we aren't too sure what to do with it, so we keep it hidden.

Even Christians who have been living for God and going to church for a long time may not fully understand what finding and owning this treasure looks like. We're happy going to church and happy saying that we're saved. But the true power of that hidden treasure stays buried.

I came to the point of realizing that it was time to buy the whole land, my whole life, and let that treasure affect every part of it. Sold! I made the decision that if God could answer my prayers in one area of life, He could do it in every area.

If you think of your whole life as being a farmer's field, you will realize that it's going to take effort and work to have good soil that produces the good things you plant in it. You must protect it from pests that come to steal or ruin the crop. You must pluck out the weeds that try to grow. You must tend to the whole field and not let the grass get overgrown so that the crop remains healthy.

In my life, I started to see how I could believe God's Word for healing in my body. No matter what opposition came my way, I could get the answers and the power of God to fix and overcome my challenges.

Well, that power to change my body and health from the inside-out is the same power of God that wanted access to change every part of my life—my marriage, my children, my finances, my relationships, and my ministry.

I was giving that treasure access to every part of my life, not just the hidden and the unseen but the physical and the everyday.

There are promises and scriptures that pertain to every area of life. If I could stand on the scriptures about health and healing and declare them over my body to see physical changes, I could do the same thing for all the other areas of my life. Financial scriptures, mind and thinking scriptures, love of God scriptures, child of God scriptures, peace and joy scriptures... the list is endless.

God became my everything. He was where I was going to find life, live life, and enjoy life. With this new revelation, I chose to become stubborn in every area. It was worth selling everything I had to the God who had chosen to answer my prayer at fifteen, speak to me at eighteen, and now show me the truth about faith. I would receive everything He had and allow Him access to every part of me.

chapter seven

Healing

THE FIRST THING I USED THE TREASURE FOR CAME IN THE AREA OF healing. After all, I was desperate. I was tired of hearing negative diagnoses about my babies or my body. Instead of listening to those voices, I let the treasure be the final voice. Having a baby that no one had thought possible changed my thinking.

I had questions that only God could answer, so I went back to Bible school—the *best* Bible school: Holy Spirit school. Not only did I listen to encouraging messages, I also wrote down every scripture that spoke to my heart. There were so many.

I had already read the Bible from front to back, but now it came alive to me with hope and encouragement on every page. As my own spirit stirred inside me, I began to look at my challenges differently.

When I was pregnant, for a time I started to get heartburn. I knew this was a common symptom of pregnancy. People sometimes could take an antacid or something. But I wasn't used to the sensation and one day while lying in bed, and the heartburn crept in, my spirit's response was: *There's no heartburn in heaven.* I kind of chuckled at the thought. I had never thought like this before, but did it ever make sense!

I got so excited that I declared this out loud. "If heartburn isn't in heaven, I don't need to have it here either! Go, in Jesus's name!"

It immediately left.

What had just happened? I started to mull over all the other things we struggle with here on the earth that don't exist in heaven.

The reason hearing this voice and speaking it was so powerful to me is that this concept is based on scripture. When Jesus was teaching His own disciples how to pray, He said, *"[Y]our kingdom come, your will be done, on earth as it is in heaven"* (Matthew 6:10).

I was overjoyed at this revelation that had just changed my thinking, allowing me to manifest healing immediately.

For some evenings afterwards, I kept getting the heartburn but doing the exact same thing. Each time, the heartburn left.

This, I believe, was a major time of testing. God wasn't bringing this heartburn on me. Rather, it kept trying to come back, perhaps because of what I had eaten, or maybe because I was having a baby with lots of hair—or so goes the old wives' tale. Regardless, I was on guard. My weapon was drawn and the heartburn could not stay.

Eventually it never bothered me again.

This same spoken statement became so engrained in my mind that I began using it for everything. If a headache tried to come on, I would declare that headaches don't exist in heaven, and it too would leave.

That may sound silly. I know a lot of people who are very affected by headaches. Sometimes headaches come from injury or lack of sleep, a lack of water, etc. But I did the same thing each time I felt a headache starting, and before I could even get out the words God would sometimes tell me where the pain was coming from.

"Christie, you didn't drink enough water today. Christie, you didn't have a good sleep last night; go have a nap. Christie, you've had too much sugar or coffee. Christie, your salt intake was through the roof!"

This Christie should really listen to the Holy Spirit!

There was a day when I went out to eat at a fast food restaurant, and that evening I had a terrible headache. Well, one week later I went to the same restaurant, probably ate the same thing, and had another terrible headache. When I asked God, He reminded me that the headaches were the result of eating that same food. So I haven't eaten there since.

I'm serious about this part of our walk with God. He has answers for us and for everything to do with us.

Danrey and I got pregnant again after our promised second child, and this time a whole new set of issues arose.[1] By the time I was pregnant with our daughter, I felt like we were winning the battles in many of these areas we had been dealing with. I was ready this time with all the Scripture possible and started making declarations the moment I thought that I might be pregnant.

I was having an enjoyable pregnancy when one day the doctor told me that the ultrasound showed a bright spot on my daughter's heart, an indicator that is normally related to Down syndrome. I was shocked by the words but didn't say a thing.

When I left the office and walked down to the van where my husband was waiting, I told Danrey about the spot they

---

1   To read more about my pregnancy experiences, check out my book *The Promised Child.*

had found. Together we declared that the reason for this spot was not Down syndrome.

I shared what had happened with my mom as well, and her response brought peace to my heart. She told me that the doctors had detected Jesus shining through the baby's heart.

For the next six months, it was hard not to connect emotionally with those words spoken over me by the doctor. I had to turn my mind from it frequently and declare God's Word—to declare His peace.

My daughter was eventually born with no signs of Down syndrome.

Not too long after the birth of our little girl, we were pregnant again. Going into the pregnancy this time, I wasn't even fazed by any cramping. I gave no thought to any concern.

During this pregnancy, there was some talk of gestational diabetes. Well, that doesn't exist in heaven, and I didn't receive it here either. Before each medical test, I was simply reminded not to eat lots of the cookies I was craving.

At this time in our lives as well, we had a lot of little children around the house and so there were lots of germs and gross stuff going around. So I took the treasure to my children. I learned about fevers and colds and prayed over my children, immediately commanding all sickness to go. Then I took care of them in the best ways I would think of. I didn't run to baby medication, which had been the norm before. Instead I watched and learned. I learned that a fever is a good thing; it means that our bodies are doing what they were created to do: fight off viruses.

We did have to bring one of our sons to the hospital for a weird cough he developed. The solution, it turned out, was for him to breathe in cold air. Wow! Some things are so simple. So when his coughing came, we would stick his head in the freezer!

What we really learn as parents is that the Holy Spirit will help us with everything. God is always there.[2]

For years I had been paying close attention to my body, my health, and the Word of God. They work together! So I was really surprised the day I realized that I had hung on to something without even recognizing that it was there. I'm not someone who keeps pain medication in my house or purse, but I did keep a medication for motion sickness when I went on a trip. Whenever I went on a plane, I took the medication right away without thinking twice about it.

> WHAT WE REALLY LEARN AS PARENTS IS THAT THE HOLY SPIRIT WILL HELP US WITH EVERYTHING. GOD IS ALWAYS THERE.

While attending a ministers conference down in Texas with my husband, I was challenged with this. During a meeting one night, the speaker prayed over everyone and declared healing for things. At one point, he called out "motion sickness."

Woah! That stopped me in my prayer. I realized that I had never even prayed about my motion sickness. I had just lived with it.

This happened during the last meeting of the weekend and we were set to head out the next day, catching two flights home. While we were packing our bags, I found an entire

---

2   To read more encouragement about parenting, check out my book *Crayons, Crumbs, and Christian Growth.*

package of motion sickness pills I had just purchased, un-opened, and stared at it. My thoughts told me that I didn't have to take one but that I could just keep them in my purse. My spirit, however, told me to throw out the whole package if I truly believed I was healed.

Those were two totally different thoughts—one safe, the other extreme.

I threw them out and didn't tell my husband what was going on. I didn't want to tell him about the struggle in my mind because I didn't want him to treat me any differently or ask questions.

When we were ready to board the first plane, the flight attendants bumped us up to a seat nearer to the front. Favour! With silly excitement bubbling up inside me, I noticed that the woman beside me was reading a book. I never read books while flying because of how it made me feel, but this time I proudly grabbed my book and read away! Meanwhile, Danrey napped.

After landing, we only had a short wait before boarding our next plane. That's when I saw a child eating an ice cream cone. I wanted one but knew I couldn't eat before a plane ride. No way could I stomach anything.

But I went out anyway and got a cheeseburger and large ice cream. Danrey had no idea what had come over me. I was so happy to eat it, and so was he.

Then we boarded our last plane, we once again got our seats bumped up—this time, right behind first class. I thought I was going to sleep, but the man sitting next to me reminded me of my dad in so many ways, and all he wanted to do was chat all the way back to Winnipeg.

When we landed, I was so excited to tell Danrey about my victory! He wasn't just amazed at how well I had done without the pills, but my attitude throughout the day. I had come out of that grave!

One of the biggest struggles we all have is managing our minds. This is a constant workplace for all of us. Problems like depression try to creep into our thoughts. I experienced bouts of depression during the years of my miscarriages. I've had to engage in a lot of self-talk to encourage myself through my insecurities.

This is probably the biggest area of healing anyone goes through. I know that the struggle is real, but the treasure is also here for us. We need to think about and ponder the realization and revelation of God in order for our faith to grow.

I had to think about this treasure I had found and come to an understanding that it can affect every area of my life—if I let it.

Dr. Caroline Leaf is one of the greatest teachers about the brain. From her, I have learned how faith and scripture work in the mind to heal our broken parts. Faith heals the wounds that words or feelings have made. Only God can produce that in us.

The more I read the Word and hear it spoken, the more I believe it. I base my decisions on what I've stored up in my mind.

I am healed. I really can't think any other way. We are the healed holding onto our healing. That may sound like a crazy concept, but the Bible says that Satan *"comes only to steal and kill and destroy; I have come that they may have life, and have it to the full"* (John 10:10). This means that we don't lacking anything. God already said in His Word that we have been healed. Long ago, He called it finished, so we should too.

This also means that we, with our actions and words of faith, have to hold on to our healing and fight the good fight of faith (I Timothy 6:12).

chapter eight

Finances

When I began to physically apply this treasure I found to my own body, so many changes occurred in my life. And I hear so many testimonies about healing that it's a no-brainer for me.

I am healed. Period.

I had made that decision in my mind and started to look at other areas of my life. If God's Word was true in the area of healing, I figured it must be true in every other area as well.

I previously wrote a book called *That's My House* which goes into great detail about our faith journey in the area of our finances. For ten years, we experienced so many pivotal learning experiences, miracles, and teachable moments that I had to share about them. But all in all, what happened is that we took the same formula we had developed for our health and healing and applied it to our finances.

God is our provider. Period.

Sometimes it's hard to focus on multiple areas of our lives at once, so I feel as though God has brought them to us one at a time! He put it on our hearts that He is our provider just like He is our healer. There's no difference.

Danrey and I were never ones to think that God cared about our finances. I mean, He cared about other people and helped them, but we thought we were to work and figure it out ourselves. We assumed that every financial burden we carried was our own fault and we should leave God out of it. He had bigger things to deal with. We were happy to see Him heal us at first but didn't want to ask for too much more.

We were wrong in our thinking about God and the treasure He had given us. We began to hear testimonies about financial blessings, provision, and all types of impossible situations. It became the norm to expect this sort of thing to happen in our lives.

Because we never had wealth growing up, we learned quickly to give God control in that area of our lives. I say we learned this *quickly* because we had so much pressure on us from every creditor. Something had to change fast.

I know it's difficult for some people to understand that God wants to be their provider. In this world, the word status means so many different things to so many different people. And we feel pride when it comes to controlling our finances because we're the ones working hard to earn it. We make our paychecks and want to take credit for the good breaks when they come.

I strongly believe that when a person is able to release their money matters over to God, they will experience significant breakthrough in their lives. That's what happened to us.

Tithing is the biggest test for people, especially here in the western world. We ask ourselves, "Why would I want to give money to a church when they don't handle it properly, or they don't handle it the way I think they should?" I hear this a lot. What people don't realize is that the moment you decide to give, God sees your heart (your faith) and He receives it first.

Then it's important to give where He leads you to give. Being financially invested in a church will benefit you more than you expect. You're helping to spread the gospel. You're helping others get delivered and set free. You're trusting that God is leading the church to make the right decisions. Trust is the biggest issue. Letting go and letting God doesn't seem to be a popular decision.

> IT'S IMPORTANT TO GIVE WHERE HE LEADS YOU TO GIVE. BEING FINANCIALLY INVESTED IN A CHURCH WILL BENEFIT YOU MORE THAN YOU EXPECT. YOU'RE HELPING TO SPREAD THE GOSPEL. YOU'RE HELPING OTHERS GET DELIVERED AND SET FREE.

Even as a teenager, I saw the importance of giving. So once I became an adult, I never stopped. The problem Danrey and I had was that we were giving without realizing *why* we were giving. We forgot that we were giving to God and not an organization. We forgot that God receives it first, and so we did it without thinking. We didn't pray over our giving together. We didn't take time to ask God about it, or whether we should give any more. We gave blindly.

We also didn't recognize those times when He was showing us His provision. We just gave ourselves a pat on the back for working hard or saving well.

In our marriage, we put all the pressure on ourselves, and we paid a high price for the stress that came with that.

Praise God that our blinders came off.

We went through a time of terrible debt and frustration and then started our own church and our own business. We saw blessing after blessing in our finances. We stand in a position today where we believe for greater things in our lives because we don't limit ourselves. God is unlimited in His resources. He gives us the desires in our hearts, which means that the desires I have are inside me for a reason. God is drawing them out!

God's Word started to come alive to us. Many times, we only had $10 and needed to spend it on gas. We would pray over it, use it, and then see His hand at work. Provision would come. I never hung my head in shame during those times. In fact, those are the periods when my faith grew the most. And honestly, I love seeing God come through.

If we never went through these financial challenges, we wouldn't have known the great promises of our God.

We don't give God enough credit. He says that He has great plans for us and that He blesses the work of our hands. He says that whatever we sow, we reap (Galatian 6:7). We just have to realize who our source is. God may have led us to the job or position we have, but He is still the source. He gives us the grace to carry out the assignment He has us in right now.

We took the treasure we found and brought it into the finances we had. We then believed that all the scriptures that talk of God's provision were for us, right now.

I have an old, tattered notebook in which I wrote out more than fifty scriptures. I've been carrying it now for about ten years. I still declare these scriptures; I share them, and I believe every one of them. Some of them are written on my vision board. I created that vision board to be filled with my goals and dreams. On it are the many seeds my husband and I have sown into other ministries and people.

If we don't have provision for something we want, or something we're already doing, then we must believe and give a financial seed (this is over and above our tithes). According to Mark 11:24, we believe that we will receive what we've asked for in prayer, and we believe that God is leading us to that harvest.

God isn't looking for how much money you give, though; it's the heart behind the gift that makes the difference.

When I choose to believe, it's like a switch goes off and I become a cheerful giver!

Giving wasn't always a cheerful thing for me. Sometimes it has felt more like trying to squeeze toothpaste out of the container. But faith without works is dead (James 2:17). I don't want dead faith, a dead relationship with God, or a dead complacent life. That's what I had before. I want to live life believing and receiving *all* that God has for me, so that He can use the finances He has given me to steward at any time!

I know that He is taking care of me and always will, no matter what the economy or the markets say. God is my provider.

chapter nine

Ministry

WHEN WE FOUND THE TREASURE AND WENT ABOUT THE PROCESS of bringing it into every area of our lives, it began to affect our ministry. We had been working in a church for nine years when the "suddenlies" started to take place. Suddenly we were having a baby. Suddenly our health was improving. Suddenly we purchased my parents' home. Suddenly our speech and outlook changed. Suddenly people started to ask questions. We physically saw many changes occurring.

> YOU ARE THE MINISTRY. YOU ARE THE LEADER WHOM PEOPLE ARE LOOKING TO FOLLOW AND LOOK UP TO. YOUR MINISTRY IS ANYWHERE YOU ARE AND IN EVERYTHING YOU DO.

That's when we were faced with yet another life change. We were free, God was moving in our lives, and we were so happy to share the good news with everyone around us. Although it didn't make sense to everyone around us, God gave us the vision to start our own church. This was a huge move for us. We were nervous, excited, and passionate to share the good news, the Gospel, with everyone who wanted to listen!

You may think that ministry is just church work, but God can use you anywhere. You are the ministry. You are the leader whom people are looking to follow and look up to. Your ministry is anywhere you are and in everything you do.

My husband and I were always athletes, from playing to coaching volleyball and basketball almost all our lives. After about a year of marriage, with us both out of college and working at the church a lot, I had prayed, giving God my volleyball playing and choosing to make church my priority. I missed volleyball since graduating from college and coaching just wasn't working out. I felt like I had given up something huge in my life.

That night, God gave it back to me. While at home alone one day, God whispered to me, *"Christian Women's Volleyball League."* He was inspiring me to build my own league!

So I pursued the idea and within a few months I had a new league up and running. My main reason for starting the league was to somehow use it as evangelism. I had friends who wouldn't come to church, but they would come out to play volleyball. So we would pray with all the athletes before each game.

That first year was so successful. Only four teams registered, with the players coming from other churches or groups, and most of them shared the same vision. They loved to play volleyball and wanted to do so in a fun, Christ-centred environment where they could bring their friends and family. We had referees, trophies, wind-ups... and testimonies.

That first season started a fifteen-year journey through the adventure of running my own sports league. In those years, we prayed with all sorts of people and lived life alongside these wonderful athletes. That was my greatest reward. The gym was my church and people got to hear about Jesus every week and pray together. Some even shared testimonies and prayer requests.

These women and their families went through pregnancies with me. They got to see the ups and downs of living faith. We were doing life together!

People joined the league who had never stepped foot in a church before. Some of these people even made their own teams and called this league their church. They loved to come; it was a different atmosphere. It was Jesus.

One woman became a good friend of mine. She had been invited one year to play for a particular team, and she came back year after year, even forming her own team.

At a game one evening, she injured her ankle very badly and had to come off the court. Out of boldness and love, I went to her and prayed. She thanked me and then was happy to let me know the following week that she had been healed. Immediately after the game when the injury had occurred, she hadn't even been able to walk. But by the next evening, she was able to go dancing at a social. She thanked me when she saw me next and told me that it had been the prayer. God had healed her.

Another evening, this same friend didn't feel too good and had an anxiety attack on the court. She left the game and I followed her out of the building, where she let me know that she was going through a lot of things and just needed a moment to catch her breath.

I put my hand on her and prayed simply and quietly over her. Then I went back inside.

A few minutes later, she rejoined her team, but I kept praying for her under my breath, breaking off any oppression that was on her and commanding the enemy to flee.

Well, a few moments later something really funny happened on the court to one of the other players. My friend broke out laughing, so hard and for so long that it got all of us in the gym laughing right along with her! I knew that whatever had been trying to hold her down was now broken off. She had been released.

She came to me moments later and whispered in my ear, "I know you prayed for me."

God is only limited by our own thinking of what outreach and ministry is. God will work through you wherever you're at and with whatever you have in your hands.

During the time of this writing, we are in the middle of the COVID-19 pandemic. Although I know that God is our healer and provider and that we have nothing to fear, we are in pressured times with our church and sports outreach. The government has placed huge restrictions on gatherings, which has affected our normal outreach and income.

But I want to tell you that what the enemy means for evil, God is using for good (Genesis 50:20). During this time, even *more* people have been coming to know who Jesus is, tuning into our church livestream and attending again when things have opened a little.

Our sports have also been taken to a whole new level of outreach. We now have a kids program and God has brought the right people around us to help reach even farther during this time.

God cannot be stopped. We trust that as we give all our dreams and desires to Him, He will use them for His purpose. As we take the treasure to these different areas of ministry, we realize that God is turning everything for His glory, and all these undertakings will succeed and prosper.

Because of the testimonies I carry in these different areas of my life, it is much easier to pray and believe for other people to receive their healing, provision, restoration, and breakthroughs.

One of the biggest ministry outreaches in my life is one that came about just from sharing my testimony. After struggling with my health and having a breakthrough, I felt the desire to write my own book. I didn't expect to write four more books, but I found myself wanting to share about everything that was starting to happen in my life.

From my writing came came social media posts, making videos, and sharing online—even speaking live. That wasn't the old me. I never thought my life would be exciting or important enough that anyone would want to listen to me—that is, until God kept giving me the desire to share. Once I began to share, more opportunities came. Then more testimonies came from those who had listened to me speak. The word just spread! Now if you search for my name online, all sorts of pictures, videos, books, and a website pop up.

As I humble myself and be honest and real with God, He works through me to share His treasure. I know that I'm not the most eloquent or exciting speaker, but being able to encourage even one other person has meant the world to me. And God has encouraged many people through my sharing.

One day I heard in my spirit that God was going to take me to the nations. I got excited but then nervous because I didn't even know what that would mean.

Over the course of the following year, I became very sensitive to the word *nation*. And I know that God is causing me to be sensitive to this word because a time is coming when I will see it happen.

God is on the move! My field, where my treasure is, is bigger than I thought!

chapter ten

Relationship Restoration

SOMETIMES WHEN WE TAKE A LOOK AT OUR PERSONAL LIVES, IT'S easy to dream about all the things we would like to have or the places we would like to go. We pray and believe for the dreams and gifts that God has placed inside us. We pray about God using us to do great and awesome things.

God is working out all things in our lives for our own good. He doesn't just focus on one certain thing we're praying about; He knows how to grow us and make us whole. If I were to focus on merely one area and bring the treasure to bear on it, I wouldn't see the fullness of God. He wants to heal, fill, and restore every area of our lives. He said that He has given us life to the *full*.

In this time of seeking after God and allowing Him to teach, lead, and guide me in all these areas, I didn't specifically pray to be filled with so much restoration of my family and relationships. These are the real gems of my life.

When I chose to follow Jesus, a lot of people around me didn't know why I was doing it. The friends around me hadn't experienced the same revelation I had as a teenager, which brought me to the point of having to say no to the lifestyle choices they were making and take a big step away from them to pursue God.

Although my closest friends tried to understand, they didn't know how to digest it all, especially when I suddenly enrolled myself in Christian college and left everything and everyone behind. It was really hard for me that these people couldn't understand the choices I was making. I was sad for them—and for me. I felt like I was leaving them all behind, or maybe they were leaving me behind. I was on a different path.

In the Christian world, I heard a lot of scriptures and teachings about being unequally yoked, and I could understand this concept. But I also found great comfort in knowing that the same God who spoke to me also loved my friends. He would have to speak to them and show them the way Himself.

We continued to grow apart from each other for years. Then weddings happened, families happened, and I only kept in slight contact.

Then one day I realized that God, in His own way, was bringing about a restoration in these relationships. One of my old friends called me up one evening and cried on the phone with me. She had just found out that she had miscarried her baby. The feelings she was having were so real and painful.

After only a short time of talking, she expressed that I was the only one who she had felt would be able to understand how she felt. She had needed to talk to me and let it all out.

I got to pray for her that day. I connected with her on a deeper level than we had ever connected in our lives. I got to share my treasure with her.

Another day, a different friend called me. After beating around the bush, she finally came out and asked how Danrey and I were getting by. How was I able to be a stay-at-home mom, not having a full-time job, while having a husband who pastored and didn't make a lot of money? And even more, we owned our own home! She couldn't understand the financial peace I had.

This was another opportunity to share the treasure with a friend.

God is restoring the years that were eaten by locusts. It may have taken more than ten years to have these open conversations again, but praise God they are happening—and I didn't try to make them happen.

My family is another story.

When I was about fifteen years old, my dad found out that he had another son who lived in another province. Wow, were we ecstatic! We received a picture of him in the mail and he looked exactly like the brother I had grown up with.

> GOD IS RESTORING THE YEARS THAT WERE EATEN BY LOCUSTS.

Dad and I took a drive out to meet him and it was the most amazing experience. The little town where my new brother lived had heard about us in advance. We stopped by a local restaurant before we went to meet him and the waiter there had known we were coming!

I felt so blessed to have two brothers. We tried to have family reunions every time my new brother travelled to Winnipeg to visit us.

Well, a few years went by. By this time I had graduated and was headed off to college. That's when we learned from my dad that we had another sister, too. My dad hadn't been told about her when she was born and she had grown up in a different part of the country.

She was like me, with light red hair and freckles. Unfortunately, because of her age at the time, not to mention the distance, we didn't get to communicate with her. But she remained a piece of my heart somewhere that I wanted to connect with.

All these years later, as I write this book, it's Christmas and my dad has given me my sister's phone number. I'm excited and nervous to connect. She's been on my heart a lot lately and now I know it's time. I feel overwhelmed.

As for the treasure I've been writing about, I don't think I ever realized that I had taken it into this part of my life. I had prayed for my family but never had I thought my family would hold so many surprises and fill my heart so much.

A few years ago, my dad signed up with Ancestry.ca to find any other relatives or family connections he didn't know about. One day I got another phone call. I had a third brother! This news came during some of the busiest times of our ministry and family life, and through it all God was putting together more pieces of the family puzzle and bringing restoration.

My dad had told me not to contact or track down this third brother but instead to wait until my new brother made first contact. It turned out that this brother thought we had known about him all these years and just hadn't tried to find him. The truth, yet again, is that Dad was never told he was even born.

Soon enough, close to Christmas, I finally got the okay to contact my new brother. It was amazing to talk to him. From his Facebook profile, he looked just like my dad and other two brothers.

Shortly after connecting with him, he planned to take a trip from the small town where he lived to visit Winnipeg. What an amazing reunion we had! No words can describe how my heart felt in those moments. We even had the opportunity to celebrate two of my brothers' birthdays, since they were exactly one year and one day apart.

That reunion started an amazing journey for our whole family. The following summer, we planned to all meet up again, but this time at Dad's house. I cried often, so overwhelmed with God's love.

In the last few years, we have all tried to visit as often as we can.

I know that my family is sharing in this treasure I found. Between online church services and YouTube, every member of my family has connected with me on a different level. I pray for them and can see healing happening in their lives. God is at work in them, too, and I'm constantly amazed and surprised by the growth and blessings in our family.

Our family may not always be perfect, but now we have each other to share our love and blessings with.

chapter eleven

My Dwelling Place

THOSE WHO ARE CLOSEST TO ME HAVE THE OPPORTUNITY TO SEE and experience the treasure, but they also see and experience the growth that happens, the change that takes place, and the challenges we face. This is not an easy place to be and it's not for the weak.

The treasure is where the heart is, and the biggest part of my heart is at home. The Bible says that no evil thing shall come near my dwelling (Psalm 91)—and that's where I am most of the time. It's where I'm supposed to be able to let my guard down and relax.

Home is the best and hardest place to walk by faith. For so long, my husband and I both made our home a place where we let go, but we didn't always make it a place where we filled back up. Therefore, our home was a place of frustration, complaining, and bad attitudes. We were living the good life outside our home and just managing to get by inside.

The treasure is for our home as well. In fact, I think it should shine even brighter there. Home is a place where we are

> THE TREASURE IS FOR OUR HOME AS WELL. IN FACT, I THINK IT SHOULD SHINE EVEN BRIGHTER THERE. HOME IS A PLACE WHERE WE ARE SAFE AND PROTECTED. IT'S A PLACE WHERE THE TREASURE NEEDS TO BE MOST EFFECTIVE.

safe and protected. It's a place where the treasure needs to be most effective.

Marriage is a state in which two people become one. They join forces and choose to love, encourage, and live for God with each other. Or something like that! I wrote a whole book dedicated to the subject of marriage to try to help bring people understanding, peace, and joy where God has shown it to us.

Marriage is not easy, but it can be amazing.

Because your partner is always around, it may be hard to see the growth—to see all the treasure in your marriage. I do the same thing for my marriage that I do for any other area of my life; I see scripture in it, and then I speak that scripture. I speak what I want to see in our marriage and declare good things for my husband. This is sometimes tough to do because you're in it all the time. It's easy to get frustrated with each other, or lazy when it comes to praying together. Sometimes Danrey and I save our best selves for everyone else and then we come home and let the frustration out.

But our homes are to be safe places. If all we do there is complain instead of speaking life and worshiping God, we won't see what the treasure can do in this area of our lives.

In my book *Marriage Uncut*, I write about how my life was before we met, and then how it was when we dated, along with the blessings of getting married and the trials we faced afterwards. Thank God He was always there with us and helped us when we asked Him, although that help didn't always look the way we expected.

Home is where the rubber meets the road in our faith. If I can't have and express my faith at home, how can I have and express it anywhere else?

When we had been married seven years, I praised God and thanked Him that this would be an amazing year in our marriage, that this was His number, the year of perfection.

Well, to me, our seventh year was anything but. We went through so much frustration physically and financially, and our relationship was not good in a good place. We barely spoke and didn't even want to be around each other.

This is the year when I felt ready to leave. I had never had that in my heart before—that is, until the pressure got to be too much and all I could think about was whether to retreat. I wanted to run away from this.

The only thing that stopped me was the fact that we had a son together. I wanted everything for my son, so I tried so hard to hide my frustration with his father. I questioned God's plan for my life, His goodness, and His purpose.

I got so frustrated and hurt one evening that I prayed a last-chance kind of prayer—and to my surprise, my husband dropped to his knees. He apologized. The resistance broke. The chains that had been holding him, the lies that were being spoken inside him, all fell away. In that moment, he got clarity.

We had to work hard to get to a better place in our marriage. I remember saying to God at the end of that year, the year that I had thought would be an amazing year, a year of perfection, that in fact it *had* been a great year. It was the year when He took out all the garbage.

Wow. We still had much to work on, but now I could see our marriage differently. It had a stronger foundation. It would have to be built up, though, and it was the treasure I found that would cause that to happen.

God made our marriage so precious to me. And now I can truly say that He is Lord of it!

I also want to discuss the subject of our children. This is a big topic, which is why I also wrote an entire book about parenting!

Again, our children are the ones at home with us. They see the good and the bad times. They get the home full of worship and the home full of chaos. When one person comes home and brings a grumpy attitude with them, soon it rubs off on everyone else.

Home is where we must be on guard with our emotions and the words we speak. Giving ourselves boundaries when it comes to our actions and choices doesn't mean we're missing out on something; it means we can live free within those boundaries. People tend to say that the Bible is just a bunch of rules of dos and don'ts. It does have a lot of rules and consequences for breaking them. If you do good, you will receive good things. If you do wrong, you will receive the consequences of those choices. Sounds like parenting to me! God loves us, His children. I love my children. I don't want them playing on the road because it's dangerous and they could get hurt, not because I'm being mean.

It's a daily choice and remembrance that the treasure is within us and in our homes. We can choose to start the day off right and we can choose to start our conversations off right. We can choose to love and we can choose to forgive. We can also choose to have fun and have joy. We can *create* with the treasure within us.

We want our children to know who Jesus is—His Spirit living inside them. We should be the first ones to be an example and reflect that. I understand that this seems like a big mandate, but with God all things are possible (Matthew 19:26).

It's the daily things we do that change our dwelling places from the inside-out. God's Word says that we participate in His divine nature (1 Peter 1:3–4). So yes, it is possible to have His peace, His joy, His thoughts, and His walk in our own character that comes from and pleases God.

Our family unit is most important, which is why we must take the treasure and apply it to our families. Pray first and give it all to God, then give everyone to God and share the love of God. We just don't know who's watching and listening when we share and show the good news.

chapter twelve

Soul

WHAT IS THE SOUL? IT'S THE MIND, THE WILL, AND THE EMOTIONS. It's the most personal place inside us. And it's also the area that needs the most work and maintenance.

When I began to see that I was seeking God and putting Him first, I watched for areas of my life in which I was praying for change. I was surprised to notice that I, too, had changed. I was changing from the inside-out.

As I let the Word of God and His power into my life, I couldn't help but change. My thoughts changed—my thoughts not just towards the world and others but towards myself.

The outer is a lot easier to deal with than the inner. I used to be able to sit and list all the things I didn't like about myself. But in the course of time, I realized that those items on my list began to disappear. I was getting closer to the truth minute by minute.

I used to measure myself up to others and discounted myself for trying hard in life. Growing up, I had done my best in school and sports and managed to always come in second or third. I may have been good at things, but I was never great.

When I took my focus off competition and instead put it on my passion—in this case, my newly developed passion to share the good news—I began to see that I could excel at a whole other level. I was influencing people! They knew my name not because I had made it on some honour roll but because of the testimony I was living.

Boldness, confidence, and courage replaced my quietness, shyness, and insecurities. By becoming bold in Christ I came out of the box I had put myself in. This caused me to share the importance of Jesus and not the importance of Christie.

> By becoming bold in Christ I came out of the box I had put myself in. This caused me to share the importance of Jesus and not the importance of Christie.

Receiving this revelation about the changes taking place in me made me want to learn and grow even more. From other preachers, I learned of some great declarations I could make. I was really drawn to these statements. I copied many of them down and declared them over myself monthly, weekly, and daily.

I don't think I'm the only one who has had to deal with self-doubt, other kinds of doubt, jealousy, fear, anger, and unworthiness. I still deal with those feelings. We need to remain aware of those feelings in our lives. They are the weeds that try to grow in our field. If we don't regularly speak good to ourselves, take care of ourselves, and give grace and assurance to ourselves, the wrong things can try to consume our minds. If we ignore the maintenance that's required to keep the weeds out, they will try to choke out the Word that has been planted. That's not the Word's fault. We plant the seeds in our minds, and with our mouths, but our own wrong thinking and attitudes can choke the good that is growing.

We are made of spirit, soul, and body. Our soul is our mind, will, and emotions, all of which can be renewed! They need to agree with the spirit and live out in our body.

When we take care of our bodies, by eating right and exercising, our minds clear and we can think better. We must take this treasure inside us physically, like medicine, to let it affect our soul.

When I picture the field of our lives, this is where the tree of life is planted. What we think, we will be.

chapter thirteen

The Big Picture

. . .if my people, who are called by my name, will humble themselves and pray and seek my face and turn from their wicked ways, then I will hear from heaven, and I will forgive their sin and will heal their land.

—2 Chronicles 7:14

As I think again about this treasure I found, having realized its value and bought the land in which it was buried, I see God's purpose and plan for my life.

My life is made up of so many different pieces. It's so complex. And God used to feel and seem complex as well. But the more I sought after Him and let Him into every part of me, I realized that He is so simple. He loves me. He has made it so easy for me to find Him. He is always there to encourage me. He sees the next steps and by His Spirit is leading me into all victory.

If I want the best of the land, my land, then I need the best gardener to work with me and teach me.

Ephesians 3:20 says, *"Now to him who is able to do immeasurably more than all we ask or imagine, according to his power that is at work within us."* The promise in this scripture is that God will match all the dreams I have with the land I have been given. I might be tending to one section of my land, bettering it, but God is working on it all, helping it to stay healthy and grow.

I understand that sometimes one area of life can get heavy, and we turn our attention to it and focus on that one thing. But know that if you keep seeking Him daily and praying in the spirit, faith will take over and impart life to every other part of you as well.

We read in Mark 4:26–27, *"The kingdom of God is like a man who casts seed upon the soil; and he goes to bed at night and gets up daily, and the seed sprouts and grows—how, he himself does not know"* (NASB).

Sometimes we hear messages or listen to sermons—and if you're like me, maybe you too have made a list in your head of all the areas of your life that need help. When you start to feel overwhelmed or anxious, you abandon the mission.

Let God be the one to reveal to you the areas of life you need to tend to. He doesn't want you to feel

> LET GOD BE THE ONE TO REVEAL TO YOU THE AREAS OF LIFE YOU NEED TO TEND TO.

overwhelmed by trying to make your life better; He wants to take the heavy burdens from you. He wants you to know that He *loves* you. He loves you whether you fix all the problems or not. He loves you even if you try hard and feel like you've failed. His love for you does not change. He is good. He is love. And He has set you up to live your life in His victory and strength.

There is so much you and I can do in this world if we just value the treasure that God is. Wherever you are, He will speak to you there. Once you allow God into your life and allow Him to take over, He gives you so much mercy and grace to help you heal, grow, and thrive.

It is to God's glory that you see the treasure you have found and then *become* that treasure. He reveals things to you that are hidden from you and for you.

> . . .to him be glory in the church and in Christ Jesus throughout all generations, for ever and ever! Amen.
>
> —Ephesians 3:21

> I will give you hidden treasures, riches stored in secret places, so that you may know that I am the Lord, the God of Israel, who summons you by name.
>
> —Isaiah 45:3

> For the revelation awaits an appointed time; it speaks of the end and will not prove false. Though it linger, wait for it; it will certainly come and will not delay.
>
> —Habakkuk 2:3

> In their hearts humans plan their course, but the Lord establishes their steps.
>
> —Proverbs 16:9

> There is a time for everything, and a season for every activity under the heavens. . .
>
> —Ecclesiastes 3:1

God keeps revealing these hidden treasures throughout your life, all in His timing. As you keep seeking, learning, and spending time in the Word, God will keep revealing things to you that take you on a journey to a higher victory. Growth happens as you sow good seeds into this land of yours.

He keeps certain things hidden until we are ready to find them. Finding the treasure and realizing its worth costs something. We take steps and make decisions that will cause our character to change. Challenges will come in our lives that cause us to persevere, building our character and giving us hope.

Hope is having a confident expectation in the Word of God. To have confidence, we need to grow in the knowledge of God and His Word. As we do this, the revelation of the Word will change us from the inside out and reveal more hidden treasure. The land is Yours to steward—and you have the ability to do it well.

> *The kingdom of heaven is like treasure hidden in a field. When a man found it, he hid it again, and then in his joy went and sold all he had and bought that field.*
> —Matthew 13:44

I love that the scripture says He went *"in his joy."* Are you joyful today? When I gave my life to Jesus and decided to follow Him with every part of me, I was filled with so much excitement and joy! Joy is a fruit of the Spirit.

No matter what's going on in my life or in this world, I am reminded that I can be joyful. The same Jesus that I had found and who changed every part of my life is still with me today. I have joy, and the joy of the Lord is my strength (Nehemiah 8:10).

I want you to walk in the joy of the Lord, having the confidence that He is doing a good work in you. Let joy be your measuring stick. If you don't have peace of mind, you won't have joy. Give it all to God by thanking Him and trusting Him with your prayers and your life. Create an atmosphere of worship and choose to praise, especially when it's difficult. Your outcome will change! Don't get frustrated with yourself when things take longer than you think they should. God knows and has an amazing plan for you!

Keep up the good work. You are full of treasure, you are worth everything to God, and there is so much more to be uncovered just for *you*.

For where your treasure is, there your heart will be also.

—Matthew 6:21

About the Author

Christie Amoyo is a wife, entrepreneur, author, and mother of four children. She has served in ministry for more than fifteen years, including women's, youth, children's, administration, worship, and pastoral. She and her husband Danrey have a heart for bringing encouragement through faith, which has resulted in the launch of Today's Church in Winnipeg, Manitoba, along with other outreach programs.

Christie's career plan changed as she married into ministry. Through working in a small business, which brought out her creativity in crafts and decor, she was drawn to helping young girls and women in their Christian walk. This experience quickly awakened a passion and desire to teach, inspire, and encourage others. As she saw the hand of God moving in her life, she felt an urgency to share the love of Christ. Pastoring alongside her husband has become an exciting adventure.

Christie has written four previous books all about the real-life challenges and breakthroughs she has received. She has written on the everyday challenges of healing (*The Promised Child*), parenting (*Crayons, Crumbs, and Christian Growth*), marriage (*Marriage Uncut*), and finances (*That's My House*). The Life of Faith series is designed to take those big faith-growth opportunities you have been given and let God take you to new levels of growth.

Also by the Author

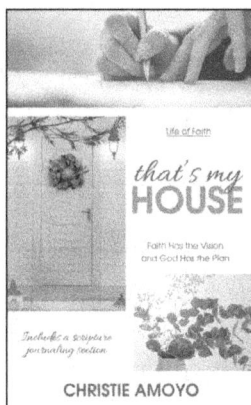

That's My House
978-1-4866-2223-8

For so long, I thought God didn't care about my family's finances. Boy, was I wrong! As I read the Bible about His provision for us, there came a shift in my head—and then in my heart. I realized that He is our *true* provider.

God has no limits and we need to believe in His provision for us in every area of our lives. No dream or vision is too big for Him—and you'll never find out what He actually wants you to do with your finances until you ask Him. Then you will be amazed at how He uses it to answer your prayers… and the prayers of others!

We have to start somewhere. It takes many little steps for us to see the fullness of what He wants for us. Your finances can be a turning point in your relationship with God. As you physically take steps to trust Him, you will see a physical manifestation of the harvest of blessings in your life.

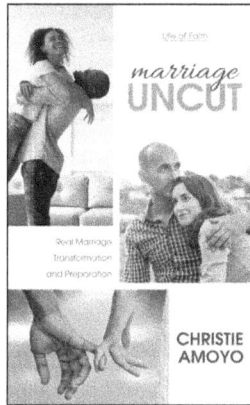

Marriage Uncut
978-1-4866-2044-9

A little girl dreams of her wedding day, not her marriage. She probably doesn't even know what the word marriage means— just how much crinoline she wants under her dress. At least this is what Christie was thinking about, not the marriage relationship, money matters, or faith decisions.

In the first half of this book, Christie shares of the real-life decisions and dramas that occurred before—and after—she and her husband said "I do." In the second half, she breaks down the pre-marriage and marriage classes her ministry shares with other couples.

Be encouraged as Christie and her husband share with you their most intimate and vulnerable experiences. Love is a choice, and through love you can forgive, hope, and give your marriage an exciting and fulfilling future.

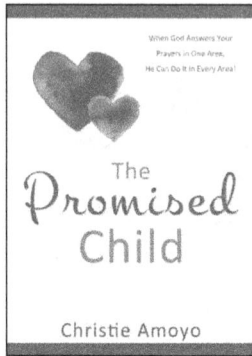

The Promised Child

978-1-4866-1649-7

Danrey and Christie Amoyo knew that they wanted to be parents, but when their happy announcement turned into the worst possible scenario they found out that becoming parents was not to be an easy path for them.

This book is a written testimony of how determination, coming from a new revelation of faith, can change lives. It will demonstrate that the promises we read about in the Bible are for us today, even if we don't yet know how they apply to the situations we're living through.

Be encouraged by the Amoyos' experience as, after years of heartbreak and loss, the Word becomes real and they put their faith first.

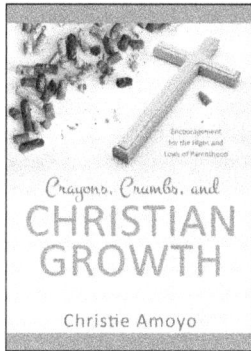

Crayons, Crumbs, and Christian Growth
978-1-4866-1714-2

Parenting children is a wonderful blessing that comes with great challenges. As you navigate the waters of parenthood, it can be easy to feel disconnected from life and your faith. You may think you are alone on this journey, and you may be frustrated trying to meet the demands all around you.

But these years can be the greatest of your life—years in which God shows you how real He is, how faith actually works, and how you can enjoy the blessings He's given you. In *Crayons, Crumbs, and Christian Growth*, Christie shares about how the trials and treasures of parenting her own children has taught her so much about who God is.

www.ingramcontent.com/pod-product-compliance
Lightning Source LLC
Chambersburg PA
CBHW071503070426
42452CB00041B/2274